STECK-VAUGHN

READ ALL ABOUT IT

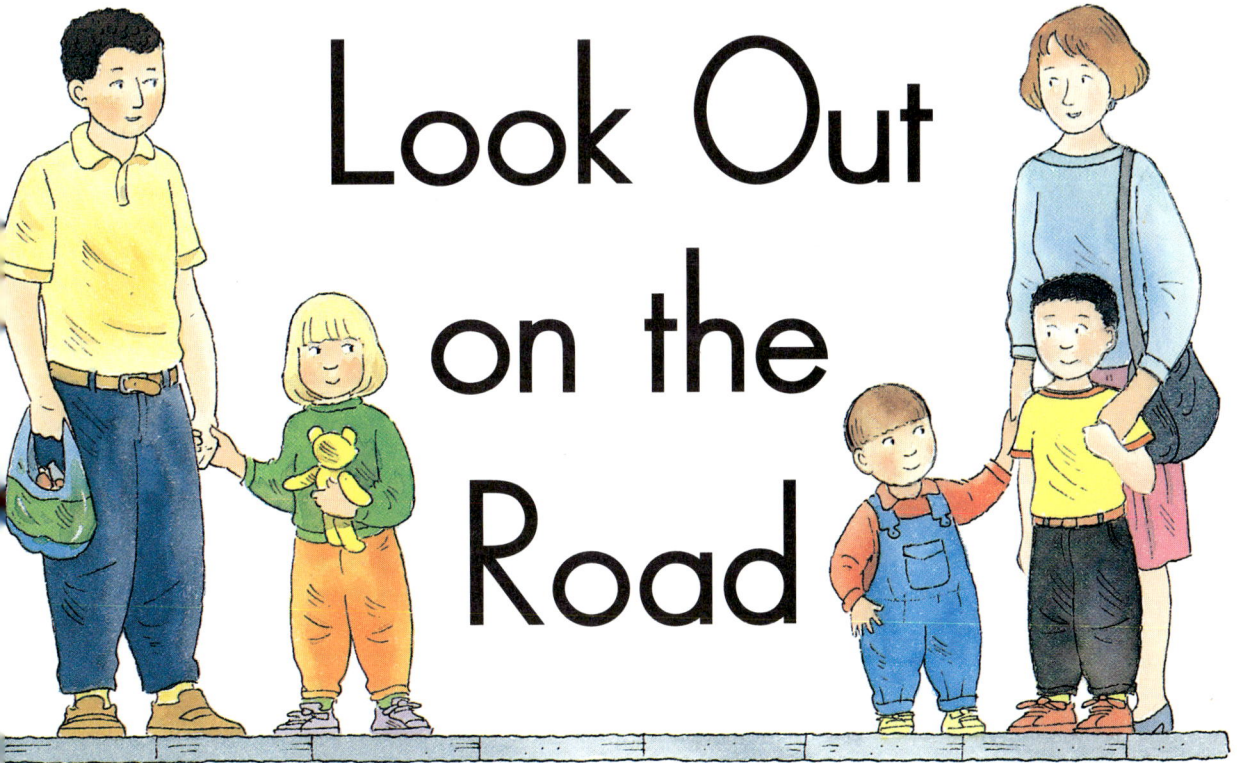

Look Out on the Road

Paul Humphrey and
Alex Ramsay

Illustrated by

Colin King

STECK-VAUGHN
C O M P A N Y
ELEMENTARY • SECONDARY • ADULT • LIBRARY

We're going shopping now.
Then we'll go for a walk in
the country.

We're in the car.

Samuel

Look Out on the Road

Acknowledgments
Executive Editor: Diane Sharpe
Supervising Editor: Stephanie Muller
Design Manager: Sharon Golden
Page Design: Ian Winton
Photography: Chris Fairclough Colour Library: cover (top right),
pages 7, 21, 23, 25, 27; Robert Harding Picture Library: cover
(middle right); Alex Ramsay: pages 9, 28-29; Quinn Stewart: cover
(bottom right), pages 13, 15; Tony Stone Worldwide: page 17, 19;
Texas Highways: cover (left).

ISBN 0-8114-3736-1

Copyright © 1995 Steck-Vaughn Company.

1 2 3 4 5 6 7 8 9 00 PO 00 99 98 97 96 95 94

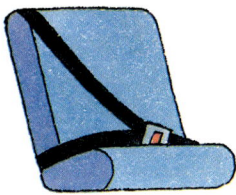

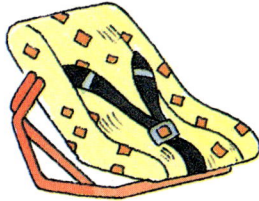

I must wear a seat belt like Mom and Dad.

I have to sit in this car seat because I'm little.

5

Here we are at the stores.

It's very busy.

There are so many people.

Always hold a grown-up's hand.
Then you will be safe.

Look at all the cars on the road.

I can see a big bus.

8

Always be careful when you are near a road.

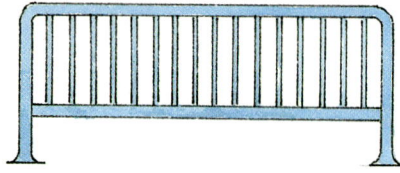

The edge of the sidewalk
is called a curb. Never
stand too close to the curb.

Let's look for a safe place to cross the road. Here is a crosswalk.

Will you press the button?

DONT WALK

PUSH BUTTON TO CROSS

PUSH
BUTTON
TO
CROSS
15 th ST.

Now we must wait for the sign to change before we cross the road.

DONT WALK

We can't cross yet.

PUSH BUTTON TO CROSS

14

The sign tells us that it's not safe
to walk across the road.

Now the sign has changed.

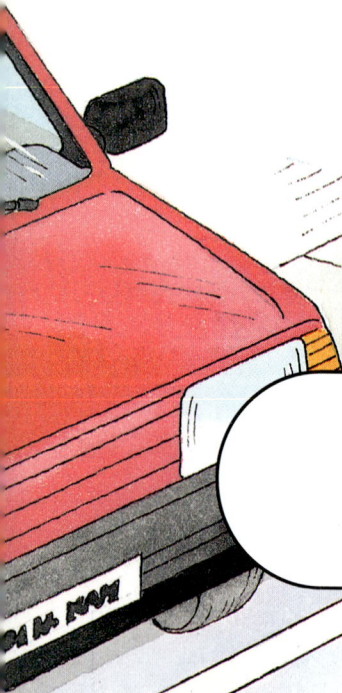

DON'T WALK

The cars have stopped for us.

It's safe to go across now.

16

WALK

Always be sure to keep looking
and listening while you cross
the road.

17

There are other safe places to cross the road, too.

The crossing guard at school stops the cars.

18

Crossing guards help people
cross the road.

19

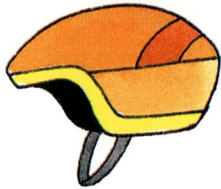

Look at the boy
on the bike.

He's wearing
a helmet.

A helmet will protect his head
if he falls off his bike.

20

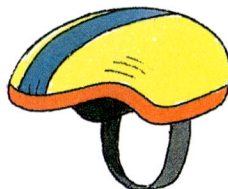

He's wearing a shiny belt.

That shiny belt helps car drivers see him.

23

Why is he putting
out his arm?

He is showing other people
on the road that he wants to
turn left.

Always walk on a sidewalk
or on the side of the road.
Then car drivers can see you.

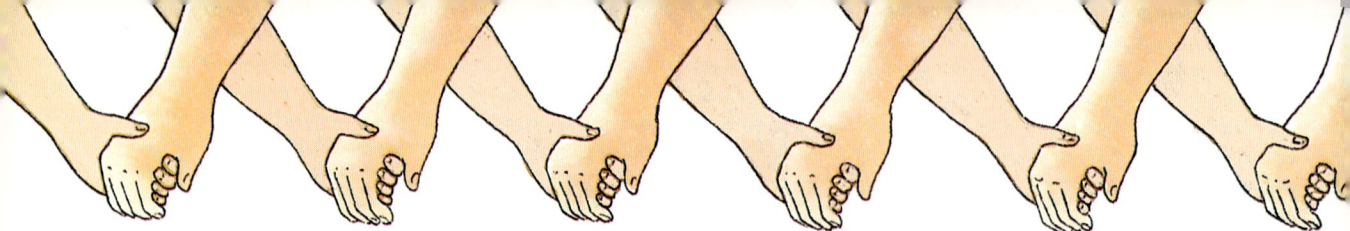

Do you remember
the rules for
crossing a
road safely?

LOOK for a safe
place to cross.

BE careful.

LOOK out for cars.

28

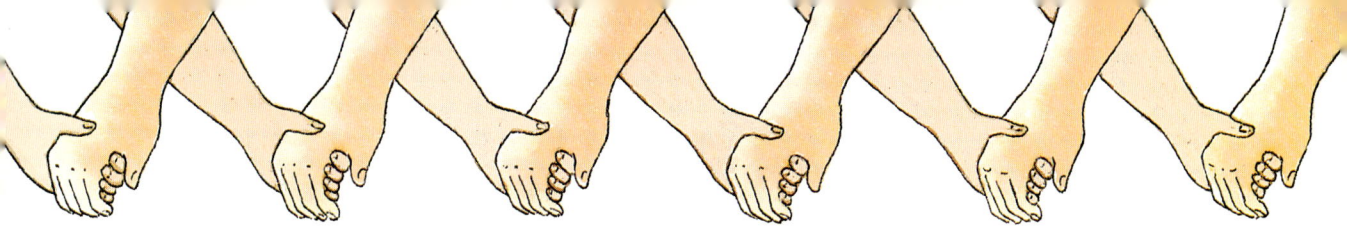

Keep LISTENING for cars
as you cross.

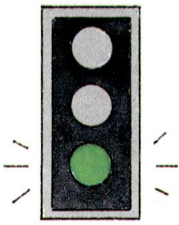

Look at the picture below.
Which people are being smart?
Which are not being smart?

Index

READ ALL ABOUT IT
SOCIAL STUDIES
STECK-VAUGHN
LEVEL A

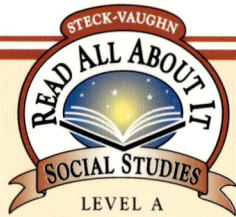

The books in the *Read All About It* series form a unique collection of first information books. Each book invites beginning readers to explore a science or social studies topic.

Social Studies/Safety Collection
People Everywhere
What People Do
Homes Around the World
Clothes From Many Lands
Watch Out for Strangers
Look Out on the Road
Safety at Home
Look Out by the Water
In Grandma's Day
In Dad's Day
Old and New
Looking Around
Let's Use It Again!
I'm Special!

Science Collection
Ask About Animals
The Caterpillar Story
Frog's Eggs
The Flower Seeds
It's Spring!
It's Summer!
It's Autumn!
It's Winter!
How's the Weather?
Hot Sun, Cold Water
Daylight, Dark Night
Journey to the Moon
I'll Push, You Pull
My Five Senses

STECK-VAUGHN COMPANY
ELEMENTARY • SECONDARY • ADULT • LIBRARY

ISBN 0-8114-3736-1

9 780811 437363

90000